Alexander invades India and is victorious in a battle with a local leader, King Porus. Alexander now calls himself "Lord of all Asia." Bucephalus, Alexander's horse, dies from battle wounds.

Alexander invades Egypt. He frees the Egyptian people from Persian rule and is made Pharaoh. He builds a new city in Egypt and names it Alexandria.

Alexander's army storms the Persian cities of Babylon and Persepolis.

Alexander dies at Babylon, the center of his empire. He is just 32 years old.

333 B.C. 332 B.C. 331 B.C. 330 B.C. 327 B.C. 326 B.C. 324 B.C. 323 B.C.

Alexander and King Darius III of Persia meet at the Battle of Issus. Alexander's army is victorious, but Darius escapes.

Alexander and King Darius III of Persia meet again at Gaugamela. Alexander's army wins the battle. Once again Darius escapes but is eventually murdered by his own men.

Around this time Alexander marries one of his captives, a princess named Roxane.

Alexander marries his second wife, King Darius's daughter Statira, in a mass wedding ceremony at Susa. Over 90 of Alexander's men marry Persian women.

McGraw Hill **Children's Publishing**

First published in Great Britain in 2003 by Brimax™
an imprint of Octopus Publishing Group Ltd
2-4 Heron Quays, London E14 4JP

Text and illustrations © Octopus Publishing Group Ltd 2003

This edition published in the United States of America in 2003 by
Peter Bedrick Books
an imprint of McGraw-Hill Children's Publishing,
a Division of The McGraw-Hill Companies
8787 Orion Place
Columbus, Ohio 43240-4027

www.MHkids.com

Library of Congress Cataloging-in-Publication Data is on file with the publisher.

© Octopus Publishing Group Ltd 2002

Printed in China.

1-57768-553-9

1 2 3 4 5 6 7 8 9 10 BRI 09 08 07 06 05 04 03 02

ALEXANDER
THE GREAT

By Penny Worms

Illustrated by Anthony Lewis

CONTENTS

PETER BEDRICK BOOKS

Columbus, Ohio

Birth of a Royal Baby

In the summer of 356 B.C., Queen **Olympias**, the main wife of King **Philip II** of **Macedon**, gave birth to a son. The king, who had many wives, lived with Olympias and their son, Alexander, in a white palace, high on a hill overlooking **Pella**, the capital city of Macedon. Macedon was a mountainous kingdom situated in the north of **Greece.** Even though Alexander was cared for by the palace slaves, the young prince was still very close to his mother. He lived with her in the women's quarters of the palace. As a baby, Alexander was wrapped in expensive cotton from **India** and silks from the east. As a boy, he had toy soldiers to play with, and he learned to read, write, and play music.

A WOMAN'S WORK

The main work for ancient Greek women was to make sure that their households ran smoothly. Wealthy women simply had to give orders to their slaves. Poor women had to do all the jobs around the home and work on the family farm. All Greek girls, rich or poor, were taught how to spin wool and weave cloth. Even Alexander's sisters, the royal princesses, would spend their days weaving and spinning!

Life as a Slave *

I must be the busiest slave in the whole kingdom of Macedon! I have been chosen to take care of the new prince, Alexander. The palace is huge and has many rooms. It is so different from my family's one-room home in the city. Baby Alexander is very cute but a real handful. I prepare his meals and keep him cleaned up, which is quite a big job! He slides on the stone floors and hides behind tall columns and statues. Now that he can crawl, I need eyes in the back of my head. He nearly tumbled into one of the wells in the courtyard yesterday. What a determined little boy!

* This is what a palace slave might have thought about caring for baby Alexander.

Children of middle class families had a much tougher start in life. They had little or no education, and no slaves to help at home. Boys were expected to help their fathers on the farm. Girls helped their mothers with the household chores. Families in the countryside grew much of the food that they needed on the small areas of land. Growing crops was hard work. The soil was rocky and poor, and the weather dry and hot. Few farmers owned their own oxen to pull the plow, so many communities had to share. Really poor farmers only had mules.

King Philip's Kingdom

When Alexander was growing up, Greece was not a single, united country as it is today. All the people spoke the same language and worshiped the same gods, but the region was divided into separate **city-states**. These city-states were each ruled by the **citizens** themselves. Every male citizen 18 and over was allowed to vote in elections, but women, children, and slaves were not. Regular meetings were held to allow the citizens to make important decisions and pass laws. This made each city-state a **democracy**. This way of government made the city-states feel superior to kingdoms like Macedon, who still had kings ruling over them. When King Philip came to the throne in 359 B.C., Macedon was a poor land and his people were considered barbarians, but Philip had great plans. He conquered **Amphipolis**, a city that had many gold mines, and he used the gold to train soldiers and buy them weapons. He then attacked and conquered Macedon's neighboring regions of **Thessaly** and **Thrace**. Macedon was becoming rich and strong. Philip was creating an empire.

King Philip was very successful in conquering other lands with his large, well-trained army and battle plans. Philip even developed the **Macedonian Phalanx**, a way for the infantry to attack their enemies. They would stay close together, holding sharp spears in front of them, keeping the enemy out of striking distance. During this time, the Greek city-states of **Athens**, **Thebes**, and **Sparta** had been fighting with each other and had not noticed how strong Macedon had become. Philip took this opportunity to attack the city-states. His goal was to conquer them all and unite all of Greece under him.

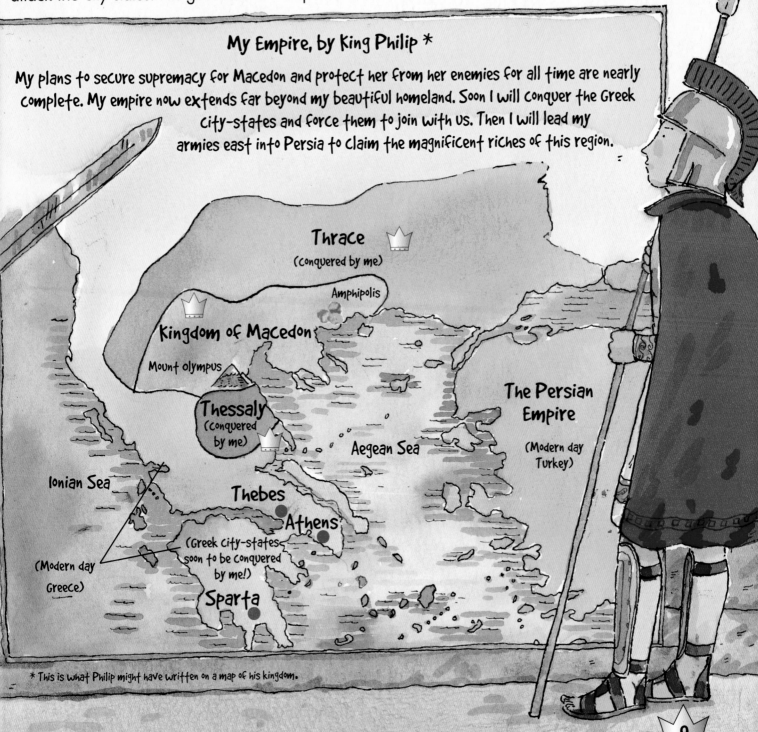

My Empire, by King Philip *

My plans to secure supremacy for Macedon and protect her from her enemies for all time are nearly complete. My empire now extends far beyond my beautiful homeland. Soon I will conquer the Greek city-states and force them to join with us. Then I will lead my armies east into Persia to claim the magnificent riches of this region.

Thrace
(conquered by me)

Amphipolis

Kingdom of Macedon

Mount olympus

The Persian Empire

(Modern day Turkey)

Thessaly
(conquered by me)

Aegean Sea

Ionian Sea

Thebes

Athens

(Greek city-states soon to be conquered by me!)

(Modern day Greece)

Sparta

* This is what Philip might have written on a map of his kingdom.

Alexander and Bucephalus

When Alexander was about 12 years old, a horse dealer brought Philip a magnificent, wild stallion. Philip asked the best horsemen in the kingdom to ride the horse to help decide whether he should buy it. One by one, riders from across the land tried to mount the horse, but it was uncontrollable and refused to be ridden. Alexander boasted that he would be able to ride the horse and asked his father if he could try. Alexander had noticed that the horse was frightened by the movements of its own shadow. Philip challenged his son—if Alexander could ride the horse, then he could have it!

CHARIOT RACING

Chariot racing was a sport in ancient Greece. Chariots were usually pulled around a racetrack by two or four horses. It was a hugely popular form of entertainment, but was dangerous - for both horses and charioteers.

My Best Friend
by Alexander *

My best friend, Hephaistion, is the son of one of my father's friends, so we spend a lot of time together. When we are not studying, we ride horses and hunt (though he is not as good as I am). We are such good friends that Hephaistion will help me when I am king.

* This is what Alexander might have said about his best friend!

Alexander walked up to the horse and spoke softly to him. He gently turned the horse around so it was facing the sun and could not see its shadow. To everyone's amazement, Alexander mounted the horse and rode off into the sun. Philip was so impressed that he bought the horse for Alexander, who named it **Bucephalus** (meaning "ox head", because of the shape of its skull). Bucephalus was always Alexander's favorite horse. They rode thousands of miles and fought many battles together. When Bucephalus died of battle wounds, Alexander held a lavish funeral for the horse, and named a city after it.

School Days with Aristotle

When Alexander was about 13, his father brought the greatest thinker of the day, the **philosopher Aristotle**, to Macedon. Aristotle was Alexander's teacher for three years, and he taught Alexander about politics and literature. Other boys went to schools. They started at the age of seven and were escorted to and from school by a slave called a **pedagogue**. The pedagogue stayed with the boys and beat them if they did not work hard. Girls did not go to school, but some were taught at home.

ANCIENT CALCULATORS

*The ancient Greeks did their math on an **abacus**— one of the earliest kinds of calculator. Rows of beads represent numbers. One row is the ones, another is the tens, another is the hundreds, and so on.*

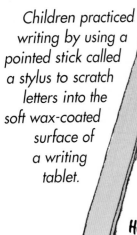

Children practiced writing by using a pointed stick called a stylus to scratch letters into the soft wax-coated surface of a writing tablet.

My Tutor Aristotle, by Alexander *

Aristotle is a great tutor, but his lessons are really tiring and he never stops walking back and forth! Still, he is a real genuis, dedicated to trying to make sense of our world through study, thought, questioning, and argument. He has inspired my love for the writings of our great Greek playwrights and poets. He has even given me his copy of the "Iliad," Homer's thrilling account of the Trojan wars. I've already read it tons of times, and I carry it with me everywhere!

* Alexander might have written something like this at school.

Boys spent the first few years at school learning to read, write, and count. They had music lessons, too, and learned to play the flute (**aulos**) and the lyre (**kithara**). When they were in their teens, boys took part in athletics and were taught wrestling and boxing. Before they left school at 18, they also studied the art of public speaking.

GREEK ALPHABET

This is the classical Greek alphabet that Alexander would have studied. The word alphabet comes from the first two letters, alpha and beta. It formed the basis of the 26-letter Roman alphabet this book is written in.

A	**Alpha**
B	**Beta**
Γ	**Gamma**
Δ	**Delta**
E	**Epsilon**
Z	**Zeta**
H	**Eta**
Θ	**Theta**
I	**Iota**
K	**Kappa**
Λ	**Lambda**
M	**Mu**
N	**Nu**
Ξ	**Xi**
O	**Omicron**
Π	**Pi**
P	**Rho**
Σ	**Sigma**
T	**Tau**
Υ	**Upsilon**
Φ	**Phi**
X	**Chi**
Ψ	**Psi**
Ω	**Omega**

The Olympic Games

Every four years, a spectacular sporting event took place in Greece at **Olympia**. It was called the **Olympic Games** and the finest athletes from all the city-states met to honor the gods by competing against one another. Their aim was to see who could run the fastest, throw the furthest, and beat the very best from other city-states. A winning athlete received a crown of olive leaves cut from a sacred tree. More important than this prize was the chance for an athlete to take glory back to his city-state. Winning athletes were treated like heroes on their return home.

CITY GYMNASIUM *

• Stay healthy • Please the gods • Ideal training for soldiers
• All the latest equipment • Open daily sunrise to sunset • Free wine and bread for all members

Running track (no rocks or chariot ruts)
Javelins (new lightweight designs)
Discus (stone and bronze available)

Slaves (for boxing and wrestling practice)
Chariots (horses provided—one piece of gold to be given as a deposit)

* If there were gymnasiums in Alexander's time, this is what they may have offered to their members.

Even wars between the city-states were stopped or postponed so that the Olympic Games could take place, and competitors and spectators could travel safely to the event. On the opening day, all the athletes went to the temple of **Zeus** (the king of the gods) where they swore to abide by the rules. Then the games began. Thousands of men from all over Greece flocked to the games to watch competitors throw the javelin and discus, race horses and chariots, box, and wrestle. All the athletes competed in the nude, except for the **hoplite** soldiers who had to run in full armor! Women and slaves were not allowed to attend and this particularly angered the girls of Sparta, who were excellent athletes. They risked being thrown off a cliff if they disobeyed the rules of the Olympic Games, though.

Olympic Champions by Alexander *

Soon it will be time for the Olympic games to be held again. I'm hoping that the Macedonian athletes will win lots of the events. When I am older, I plan to compete in the games. My horseback riding skills are now so good that I am sure I will win an olive crown and bring back glory to Macedon! The Games last for five days:

DAY 1 – Running events

DAY 2 – Pentathlon (five events of running, wrestling, long jump, javelin, and discus)

DAY 3 – Horse racing

DAY 4 – Chariot racing

DAY 5 – Boxing and wrestling

I know that to compete and honor the gods I must be fit and healthy, so I will train hard every day and continue to practice my horseback riding skills.

* Alexander might have thought this about the Olympic Games.

Food and Drink

As Alexander got older, he spent more time with his father, whenever Philip was home from war. The king loved to hold parties in the palace. Only important male guests were invited, and the eating and drinking would take place in a special dining room. The guests would be treated to plates of wild boar and deer, fried squid, cheese, olives, salads, and bread. Bread was eaten daily by most Greeks, whether they were rich or poor. It was made from wheat or barley flour, and was coarse and heavy.

King Philip's Feast *

Octopus tentacles sliced and boiled in olive oil,
Macedonian goat's cheese,
wild boar with garlic and onion,
rabbit cooked with turnips and beans,
sprinkled with fresh herbs from the mountains,
and locally caught tuna fish.

SIDE ORDERS

Hard-boiled eggs,
fresh local peas,
olive oil with bread for dipping,
sweetmeats of finest sesame seeds rolled in honey,
melon and pomegranate surprise,
wine grown in the king's vineyard
and stepped on by the cleanest
feet in the region.

* This is what the menu at Philip's banquet might have looked like!

WINE

Wine was a favorite drink in Greece, whether you were rich or poor, though the drinking vessels were different. Glass was very expensive so only the wealthy could afford to drink from glass goblets. Ordinary people had goblets made from clay baked hard in an oven.

OLIVES AND OLIVE OIL

The goddess **Athena** is said to have brought olive trees to Greece. The olives were either eaten or pressed to make oil for cooking and for pouring on salads. The oil was also burned to create lighting in houses and was used as a beauty product, rubbed into the skin to make it smoother and softer.

At every one of Philip's parties, the wine flowed freely. All Greek wine was so thick it had to be strained before drinking. Other Greeks mixed their wine with water, but the Macedonians preferred theirs undiluted—getting extremely drunk was a common occurrence at a Macedonian party! To complete the feast, the guests were offered delicious sweets made from dates, figs, nuts, and honey while being entertained by acrobats and musicians. After the meal, the men would stay to drink even more wine and have important discussions. These after-dinner talking and drinking sessions were known as **symposiums**.

17

Dressing Up for the Theater

Greek men loved going to the theater, and it is likely that Alexander attended regularly with his father, sitting in the front row in the best seats. There were open-air theaters in most cities in Greece and even the poor could afford this popular form of entertainment. The tickets were inexpensive and sometimes free, as wealthy patrons and politicians would pay for the actors to put on a play. When the play started, the **chorus** would enter the circle in front of the stage. As the chorus told the story, speaking in unison, the actors would perform behind them on the stage. The actors wore masks and changed them to become different characters, or to change their mood from happy to sad.

THE ORCHESTRA

Musicians accompanied the performance playing flutes, pan-pipes, harps, and lyres.

TODAY AT THE PELLA THEATRE

MEDEA by Euripides (a tragedy)

AGAMEMNON by Aeschylus

THE CLOUDS
by Aristophanes (a comedy)

OEDIPUS THE KING by Sophocles

Greek actors were always male. The
younger boys would play the female parts
by wearing wigs. The actors would speak
their parts and sometimes sing them. The
plays were usually comedies or tragedies.
The most popular by far were the tragedies,
the sadder the better! A visit to the theater was
a good opportunity for rich Greek families to dress up in their
finest clothes and show off their wealth. Even poor people
would wear their best tunics, although they would probably be
made of finely spun wool, not silk or cotton.

ANCIENT GREEK FASHION

The ancient Greeks paid
a great deal of attention
to their clothing and
hairstyles. Both men and
women wore white or
brightly colored tunics
fastened at the shoulder
with a brooch. Rich people
wore gold and silver
necklaces and earrings,
while the poor wore
jewelry made of bronze.
Hair was curled into the
latest styles and makeup
was used by both men
and women to cover
unfashionable suntans.

Alexander: Regent and King

At 16, Alexander was left in charge of Macedon as **regent**, or acting ruler, while Philip went away to war. Everyone admired Alexander's intelligence, hunting skills, and horsemanship, and he quickly proved himself as a leader and **general**. On receiving word that there was a barbarian rebellion east of Macedon, Alexander led an army to the barbarians' largest city and crushed the rebels. Philip was so impressed with his son that, two years later, he put Alexander in command of the **cavalry** in the **Battle of Chaeronea**. Alexander's bravery in leading his men straight into the enemy ranks helped Philip to win this decisive battle against Athens and her allies. Philip was now the ruler of most of Greece, but just as he reached the height of his power, he was murdered. Alexander was just twenty years old.

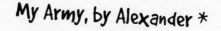

My Army, by Alexander *

I have gathered together the very best fighters from all over Greece.

- 30,000 foot soldiers from Macedon, Greece, and the Balkans.
- 5,000 cavalry from Macedon and Thessaly.
- Archers from Crete.
- Scouts from Thrace to keep watch for the enemy.
- Artists, poets, and writers to record my achievements.
- Workers to lay out our camps.
- Grooms to care for the horses and mules.
- My servants.

Hephaistion and Bucephalus are with me.
How can I lose? I will soon be the leader of a huge empire with peace and equality for all.

* This is what Alexander might have written about his army.

To become the new king of Macedon, Alexander had to be accepted by the army. This was not a problem as they already loved him. He was hailed king on the day of his father's death. He said, "Nothing has changed except the name of the king!" Some Greek states, though, rebelled against being ruled by a young Macedonian king. Alexander was ruthless. He crushed every rebellion and finally united Greece. When his father's most recent wife and her baby were murdered, it was believed that Alexander had been involved. No one would come between Alexander and the throne of Macedon.

MACEDONIAN PHALANX

Philip's success in battle was partly due to how he trained his foot soldiers. Marching in rows, the rear troops held their 19.5 ft (6 m) long spears upright while the front soldiers held theirs out in front of them. In this way, they could easily spear the enemy, but from a safe distance!

Oracles and the Gods

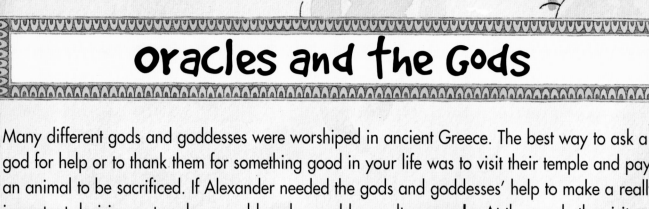

Many different gods and goddesses were worshiped in ancient Greece. The best way to ask a god for help or to thank them for something good in your life was to visit their temple and pay for an animal to be sacrificed. If Alexander needed the gods and goddesses' help to make a really important decision or to solve a problem, he would consult an **oracle**. At the oracle the visitor paid to ask the gods a question. Surrounded by burning incense and in a deep trance, the high priestess, or **Pythia**, would communicate directly with the gods. The Pythia's answer was usually complete gibberish, but interpreters were on hand to explain the meaning of the message. Alexander visited the oracle at the temple of **Apollo**, in **Delphi**, before he invaded **Persia**.

ATHENA

Each of the gods in ancient Greece had their own roles and were worshiped in their own temples. The temple, called the **Parthenon**, *in Athens was built for the goddess Athena, daughter of the king of the gods, Zeus. Athena was the goddess of wisdom and warfare and also the patron goddess of Athens, which was named in her honor.*

Meet the Ancient Greek Gods

ARTEMIS was the goddess of the moon, hunting, and small children. She used silver arrows and could out-shoot any mortal.

POSEIDON was the god of the sea and of earthquakes. He didn't live on Mount Olympus but under the ocean in an underwater palace, where he watched over sailors and sea creatures.

APHRODITE was the goddess of love, desire, and beauty. She could make any man or god fall in love with her.

HEPHAESTUS was the god of craftsmen and blacksmiths. He made weapons for the gods.

APOLLO was the god of sunlight, crops, and music.

DIONYSUS was the god of wine and grapes.

The ancient Greeks believed that their twelve most important gods lived on **Mount Olympus**, in the north of the country. Zeus was the king of the gods and god of the heavens. When people heard thunder they believed that Zeus was angry at something on earth. He was all-powerful and a master of disguise, often coming down to earth in the form of a bull or a swan. His queen was **Hera**, the goddess of women and marriage. The gods behaved just like people on earth— they fought and fell in love, and would often meddle in the lives of mortal people.

Alexander's campaigns

Now that Greece was united, Alexander turned his attention to the Persian Empire to the east, ruled by King **Darius III**. Persia had successfully invaded Greece in the past, but now it was time for the Greeks to strike back. Alexander marched east, winning battle after battle. Finally, in 333 B.C., he came face to face with King Darius III on the battlefield at **Issus**. Alexander's tactics and bravery helped him win the battle with the loss of only a few hundred men. Darius had escaped, though. Two years later they met again. This time Darius had even more men, with horses, chariots, and elephants. Darius and his generals were so confident of victory, they had brought their families along to watch. Darius even chose the battleground, at **Gaugamela**, in modern-day Iraq.

HOPLITE SOLDIERS

Among the ranks of Alexander's army were the Greek foot soldiers called hoplites. Wearing bronze leg-guards and breastplates and carrying either swords or spears, these famous fighting men marched shoulder to shoulder towards the enemy with their shields raised, chanting their battle songs.

Battle Timeline

– 334 B.C. – Alexander and his army left to invade Persia.

– 333 B.C. – Alexander's army won their first battle with King Darius III at Issus. Darius escaped.

– 332 B.C. – Alexander freed Egypt from Persian rule, became pharaoh, and built a city in his honor, called Alexandria.

– 331 B.C. – Alexander defeats Darius III at Gaugamela.

– 330 B.C. – Alexander attacked the Persian cities of Babylon and Persepolis, where they found large amounts of silver and gold.

– 326 B.C. – Alexander attacked King Porus in India. Alexander's horse, Bucephalus, died, and Alexander built and named a city in his honor in India.

The Persians were disappointed yet again. Alexander's superior leadership led the Greek army to victory. Once again Darius escaped, but the Persians had lost faith in their king and he was eventually murdered by his own men. Alexander was now leader of the whole Persian Empire. In 326 B.C., Alexander marched further east and invaded the strange and unknown land of India. This time the Greek army faced an entirely new and terrifying foe—the specially trained war elephants of King **Porus**, who ruled part of India. Although Porus's army was very strong with more than 100 elephants, the brilliant young general was once again victorious. Alexander now called himself "Lord of all Asia."

Alexander's Marriages

Alexander continued to push east, capturing more land and people. He had fallen in love and married one of his captives—a princess named **Roxane**, from **Bactria**, an area to the northeast of the Persian empire. Alexander pressed on into India and conquered many cities until his men reached breaking point. They had invaded India during the rainy season, and Alexander's soldiers were tired of marching through floodwaters full of dangerous snakes and crocodiles. They had been away from Greece for almost ten years, and they wanted to go home. Alexander reluctantly agreed, and the Greek army headed back to Persia. When Alexander returned to the city of **Susa** there was unrest among the Persian people. To promote harmony between East and West, he held a mass marriage ceremony.

Roxane *
(Alexander's first wife)

My real name is Roshanak, meaning "little star." Alexander thinks I am very beautiful and he fell in love with me as soon as he saw me. I was just 16 when we were married, and I was delighted to soon become pregnant. Sadly, our baby died before it was born. I bravely followed Alexander to India.

Statira *
(Alexander's second wife)

I was originally named Barsine, but I took my mother's name of Statira when she died. I was about 15 when I married Alexander. I needed to find a husband because I have no father to support me and cannot earn a living for myself. Although Alexander is responsible for my father's death, I trust him to be a strong and brave husband to me.

* This is how Alexander's wives might have introduced themselves.

Alexander took a second wife, **Statira**, who was King Darius's daughter. Hephaistion married Statira's sister, and ninety other high-ranking men in Alexander's army were ordered to marry Persia's finest ladies. At the mass wedding ceremony all the grooms sat in seats arranged in rows. After a banquet, the brides came in and sat next to their husbands. Each groom then took hold of his bride's right hand and kissed it. Alexander was the first to begin, with his men then following his lead. Over the course of time, 10,000 Macedonian soldiers married Persian women and Alexander even took a third wife, **Parysatis**, the daughter of another Persian king.

Death of Alexander

In 323 B.C., Alexander went back to Babylon, now the center of his empire. He started to make plans to conquer more lands in Arabia and North Africa. His best friend, Hephaistion, had died the year before. The summer was hot and humid, and Alexander suddenly fell ill with a fever, possibly malaria. His generals were waiting for the orders to put his new plans into action but when they heard nothing, they knew something was wrong. Realizing that Alexander was close to death, his generals asked him who was to inherit his empire. Alexander just said, "Whoever is the strongest." A few days later he died, at the age of 32.

THE NEW KING

*Alexander's first wife, Roxane, was pregnant when Alexander died. She had a son who became King **Alexander IV**. The young boy shared his crown for a while with Alexander's half brother, but he was murdered in the power struggles that followed Alexander's death. The alliances that Alexander had built eventually crumbled and his empire was torn apart.*

THE LEGACY OF THE ANCIENT GREEKS

The ancient Greeks have influenced many aspects of our lives today. Ancient art and architecture inspire us, and many modern governments are based on the Greek idea of democracy. An evening at the theater is still a popular pastime, with modern theaters based on the ancient Greek design. And every four years athletes from across the world compete at the Olympic Games for medals and glory!

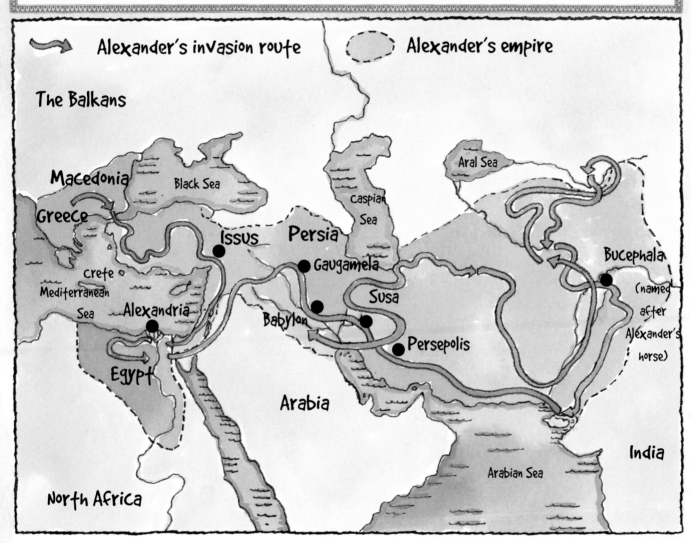

At the time of his death, Alexander's empire extended 3,000 miles, from Greece to India. Greece was united and Alexander was regarded by the Persians and Egyptians as their leader. His huge army was made up of men from many different races, all prepared to fight under him. The Greek language and currency were used throughout the empire and many new cities had been built and named **Alexandria** in his honor. Even today the Egyptian city of Alexandria is still the second largest in Egypt and the country's main port—just as Alexander had planned. The building of such a vast empire was an extraordinary achievement, and the young Macedonian king would be known throughout history as Alexander the Great.

Glossary

ABACUS A calculating machine that uses beads.

ALEXANDER IV Alexander the Great's son.

ALEXANDRIA An Egyptian city built by Alexander and named in his honor.

AMPHIPOLIS A place to the east of Macedonia.

APHRODITE The Greek goddess of love, desire, and beauty.

APOLLO The Greek god of sunlight, crops, and music.

ARISTOTLE The famous philosopher, and Alexander's tutor.

ARTEMIS The Greek goddess of the moon, hunting, and small children.

ATHENA The Greek goddess of wisdom and warfare.

ATHENS A Greek city-state, now the capital of Greece.

AULOS A type of flute.

BABYLON An ancient city in the Persian Empire. Alexander died here.

BACTRIA An area in the northeast of the Persian Empire.

BATTLE OF CHAERONEA A battle between King Philip's army and the Greek city-states (including Athens). This battle finally brought the city-states under Philip's control.

BUCEPHALUS Alexander's favorite horse.

CAVALRY The part of an army that is made up of soldiers on horseback.

CHORUS A group of actors who spoke in unison and narrated or commented on the action in a play.

CITIZEN A person who lived in one of the city-states. Citizens were the only people with the right to vote.

CITY-STATE The areas that ancient Greece was divided into. Each city-state included a major city and the surrounding countryside.

DARIUS III The king of the Persian Empire.

DELPHI An ancient Greek city to the north of Athens.

DEMOCRACY A system that allows ordinary people to have a say in the running of their country.

DIONYSUS The Greek god of wine and grapes.

GENERAL A leader of an army.

GREECE A southern European country, with coastline on the Mediterranean Sea.

GAUGAMELA The name of a village close to the battlefield where Alexander met Darius III in battle, for the second time.

HEPHAESTUS The Greek god of craftsmen and blacksmiths.

HEPHAISTION Alexander's best friend.

HERA The Greek goddess of women and marriage. Wife of Zeus and queen of the gods.

HOPLITES Greek foot soldiers who carried swords or spears.

INDIA A country in Asia to the east of Greece and the Persian Empire.

ISSUS The place in Persia where Alexander and Darius III first met in battle.

KITHARA A string instrument similar to a harp.

MACEDON A kingdom in the north of Greece.

MACEDONIAN PHALANX King Philip's infantry soldiers, who marched in tightly-packed rows with long spears held out in front of them.

MOUNT OLYMPUS A mountain in the north of Greece. The ancient Greeks believed their gods lived here.

OLYMPIA A city in the west of Greece.

OLYMPIAS King Philip's main wife and mother of Alexander.

OLYMPIC GAMES An important sporting event that took place in ancient Greece every four years.

ORACLE A special shrine where visitors could ask the gods questions about the future. A high priestess in a trance would communicate directly with the gods.

PARTHENON A temple in Athens built in honor of the goddess Athena.

PARYSATIS Alexander's third wife.

PEDAGOGUE A slave who accompanied boys to school to ensure that they behaved and worked hard.

PELA The capital city of Macedon.

PERSIA An ancient empire, stretching from Greece to India.

PHILIP II The king of Macedon and father of Alexander.

PHILOSOPHER A person who asks questions about how the world works. In ancient Greece, philosophers also studied politics, human behavior, and science.

PORUS An Indian king.

POSEIDON The Greek god of the sea and of earthquakes.

PYTHIA The high priestess at an oracle.